Also by Brian J. Noggle

John Donnelly's Gold

The Courtship
of
Barbara Holt

with

Dennis Thompson Goes on Strike

Brian J. Noggle

Jeracor Group LLC
5643 South Haseltine Road, Brookline MO 65619

ISBN-13: 978-0-9832123-2-4

Contents

The Courtship

of

Barbara Holt

A Comedy in Five Acts

The Courtship of Barbara Holt

Cast of Characters

Mark Dever

English major specializing in Renaissance Lit, a would-be courtier of Barbara Holt.

Mike Quince

Mark's best friend and a college student for seven years, Mike has designs on most women, especially Jenn Walters.

Rick "Phil" Specter

A philosophy major who reasons everything out soundly—but not validly.

Todd Russell

Business administration major, son of an important local brewer. Todd has the eye of Barbara, but is interested primarily in Penny.

Barbara Holt

A biology major who has the attention and affection of Mark Dever but isn't sure if she wants it.

Jenn Walters

An English major who thinks Mark is romantic and believes that he is wooing her.

Penny Winston

Todd's on-again, off-again girlfriend.

ACT THE FIRST

Scene I

The Setting: The patio of Todd's apartment. There is a party going on in his apartment, accessible by a set of French doors upper stage left. Mike, Mark, and Rick are standing to one side.

MIKE   And then he went up and around and did one of these *(Mimics basketball movement.)* and *(Pauses.)* plunk! Right off the rim.

MARK   That's a really nice story, Mike.

MIKE   Well, how many times have you guys pressured a major NCAA star?

MARK   Minor GMC bench-warmer.

RICK   I once asked one to define the terms in an argument he was posing. He said abortion was wrong because a fetus is a potential human, and I asked him what he meant, and then I hit him with Aristotle.

MIKE   Now that's a nice story, Phil.

RICK   Well, you asked.

MIKE   I know, I know, and I'm sorry. Say, have you guys tried this nacho dip? It's un tasto de Mexico.

RICK   Sabor. Sabor de Mexico.

MIKE   Is that who makes it? It's pretty good. Check out these digs. This guy Todd lives here alone?

MARK   I guess. It's the first time I've been here.

MIKE   He's in one of your classes?

MARK   Yeah, he's in Theology and Human Nature with me.

RICK   Do you have Doctor Roover for that?

MARK   Indeed....

MIKE   Okay, we're at a party. Let's not plan our schedule for next semester right now. A patio, too. How come I don't have a patio?

MARK   Because you live in a dorm.

MIKE   And why don't dorms have patios and balconies?

RICK   It's not cost effective and the hazards of injury greatly outweigh the....

MARK   They don't want freshman getting loaded and falling to their untimely deaths. Dead students don't pay tuition.

MIKE   Try small talk, Phil. Less syllables uses less air, and you help save the atmosphere.

RICK   Nice climatic activity we've been experiencing this annum.

MIKE   Never mind. Babble some epistemology or something.

ENTER JENN AND BARBARA.

MIKE   Rowf. *(Mimics a dog pointing at the women.)*

MARK   Down boy.

MIKE I give her a.... *(Begins counting like a horse, clops his foot eight times, pauses, then once more.)* She gets the delayed nine count.

RICK   Very appealing.

MIKE   She's doo lang.

RICK   Doo lang?

MIKE   I wish she were mine.

MARK   She's okay.

MIKE   Okay? OKAY?

MARK SHRUGS.

MIKE   What's her name?

RICK   Which one?

MIKE   The fox on the right.

MARK   Oh. That's Jenn Walters. I had her last semester in Philo 103.

MIKE   Right there in Philo 103?

RICK   Philosophy 103? I wasn't aware you had German Idealism. I found Hegel's Philosophy of the Right....

MIKE   *(Thumps foot like tickled dog.)* She looked at me. She looked at me. She's crazy about me. Let's go introduce ourselves.

MARK   Introduce ourselves?

MIKE   Strike up a conversation, make some time. It's so very hard to fall head over heels in love from across a patio.

RICK   An influx of other views is often desirable when reconciling reality to one's perception.

MIKE   Maybe you'd better stay over here, Phil. Come on, Mark.

ALL THREE MEN APPROACH THE WOMEN.

MIKE   *(To Jenn.)* Excuse me, do I know you?

JENN   No.

MIKE   *(Seizing Jenn's hand and kissing it.)* That is my mistake. My name is Mike Quince, and you are...?

JENN   Hi, Mark.

MARK   Good evening, Jenn.

JENN   *(To Barbara.)* This is Mark Dever. Mark, this is Barbara Holt. I had Mark in a Philosophy class.

MIKE   Philo 103, German Idealism, right? Hegel, Husserl, and Humbug?

JENN   Oh, he told you?

BARBARA   Good to meet you, Mark.

MARK   *(Breathless.)* Hi.

MIKE   And I'm Mike Quince.

JENN   *(To Mark.)* How's your semester going?

MIKE   Fine, thanks. Almost half way done. Yours?

JENN   About the same.

MIKE   Hang on, hang on, we've gone too far without someone saying "What's your major," so I'll have to correct it. What's your major?

JENN   English, just like Mark.

MIKE   Probably not just like Mark, but that's probably a good thing. I'm a Mass Comm major myself.

RICK   This semester.

MIKE   No, really, this time I'm going to finish it.

RICK   Sure.

BARBARA How many other majors have you had?

MIKE   Counting Mass Comm?

BARBARA Yes.

MIKE   Oh, about, four. No, five. Maybe six.

BARBARA Six majors?

MIKE   I got an early start.

> *MARK TAKES A BREATH AS IF HE WILL SPEAK.*

BARBARA I'm biology myself.

> *MARK TAKES A BREATH.*

JENN   *(To Mark.)* So what do you think of Todd's place?

MARK   *(Slowly.)* It's kind of....

MIKE   Great. A patio. I was just saying I need a patio.

BARBARA   It is rather opulent, don't you think?

MIKE   Mikey likes it.

   ENTER TODD.

TODD   Mark! You made it!

MARK   Indeed, I did.

TODD   I see you've met Jenn and Barb.

RICK   Todd has not established his educational predilections.

MIKE   What did you say? Oh, right. Major check. Todd?

TODD   Business Administration with a minor in public relations and mass communications. I figured I'd start in the people business. Maybe get a job with the brewery.

JENN   You do have experience getting large numbers of college students to drink.

MIKE   Put that on your resume. Four years as partymeister. Duties included promoting and managing assemblies of alcoholic college students.

   MARK TAKES A BREATH TOWARD BARBARA.

TODD   I could try that. Well, I have to move around some. Have to take care of my managerial responsibilities.

MIKE   Show us around. Pretend it's a brewery tour. Free samples, too.

TODD   All right. Can everyone hear me? My name is Todd, and I'll be your guide tonight. We'll start off the tour with a visit to the living room, where we can sample some of our brewery's finest....

   ALL EXCEPT MARK EXEUNT SINGLE FILE.

MARK *(Slowly.)* Ay, eh, ee, oh, ah, uh, ih. Duh, Tuh, Kuh, Buh, Guh, ssss. Er. *(Normal speed.)* Nothing's wrong with the voice or vocal cords. Except that they're mine, I suppose. Talk about a full mental vapor lock. Why didn't I say anything? What could I have said? It was all being said, just by someone else. Mostly Mike. *(Paces.)* Bah-er-bah-rah. Nothing difficult in that. What's my problem?

Scene II

Same as before.

    ENTER MIKE.

MIKE Holy cow, man. She couldn't get off of you.

MARK What?

MIKE The minute we went through the door it was "How do you know Mark?" and "Does he have a girlfriend?" You lucky dog.

MARK She did?

MIKE You bet. I played you up, of course. I told her about your grand dreams of teaching Shakespeare at Oxford and living nearly destitute on a college professor's salary for the rest of your life.

MARK You told her that?

MIKE Had to make you sound as exciting as possible. She thought it was great, too. Ate it up. I even told her about you and that fourteen-year-old high school freshman you met at that party at Phil's last year when you were both smashed and ended up in a hatchback with a Mickey Mouse sheet and a jar of Vasoline....

MARK What fourteen-year-old girl?

MIKE The one with the brown eyes and went to Parkway West.

MARK What hatchback?

MIKE It must have been Steve Richter's....

MARK   What party at Rick's?

MIKE   You're right. That's where it loses credibility.

MARK   You didn't....

MIKE   You're right. I didn't tell her the stock 'him and a high school girl' story. I would've, though, if I'd have thought it would do any good.

MARK   What did she say?

MIKE   She just cooed and giggled flirtatiously, but you weren't there to flirt with, so she almost settled for me.

MARK   Zounds.

MIKE   Mark and Jennifer, in a tree, K-I-S-S....

MARK   Jenn?

MIKE   I know, what could she possibly see in you? I am far better looking, more charming, and more intelligent than you. Not to mention I am older, more sophisticated, and have a mature wit.

MARK   Mmm-hmmm.

MIKE   Dang it, it's that modesty thing again, isn't it?

MARK   When you're perfect, you don't need to be modest.

MIKE   That's what I say anyway. So you going to go for it?

MARK   For Jenn?

MIKE   Heck's pecs, I would. I guess I've made that clear enough. Say no, please say no, oh please. *(Falls to knees.)* I beg of you, pity, pity. Here pity pity pity. Good pity.

MARK   Mike....

MIKE   *(Stands up.)* Uh oh, here she comes. I'll make like a tree and fall soundlessly in the woods. Remember, flatter like a boaterfly and be like Sting. Or something like that. *(Exits.)*

ENTER TODD.

TODD   Still out here, eh?

MARK   Yeah.

TODD   Looks like woman trouble to me. *(Pauses.)* Christ, you can't figure them out. I asked Penny Winston to come, you know, the red head who sits next to me in theology. She and I have been going for a while, and she decided not to come to my party. My party. So I'm stag at my own party. Can you believe it?

MARK   *(Shrugs.)* I stagnate most of the time.

TODD   Well I can't stand it. This might be all for her. Yeah. I think it is. Come on, let's get a beer.

MARK   Maybe in a while.

TODD   Right. Catch you then. *(Exits.)*

Scene III

Same as before.

ENTER JENN.

JENN   Hi, Mark. You still out here?

MARK   Just looking at the stars.

JENN   You can hardly see them out here. In the city, I mean. Out where I live, on a clear night, you can see them all. Well, not all the stars, but a lot more than this.

MARK   I know. I've been to the country.

JENN   Really? I grew up in Republic. Just outside of Springfield. How about you?

MARK   Edwardsville mostly.

JENN   Illinois? You have no flatlander accent.

MARK   I speak in full sentences. It throws people off.

JENN   It does. I thought you were from St. Louis.

MARK   Close enough.

> *ENTER BARBARA.*

BARBARA   *(Shaking head.)* I think your friend Rick has had enough. He's putting on quite a scene....

> *MARK SHRUGS.*

JENN   Look at the stars, Barb. That one is Rigel, and Betelguese. Orion's always the first constellation I spot. See his belt and his sword? *(Points to sky.)* Those three there. Never see the dippers. Just Orion.

BARBARA   I never notice much. How un-English major of me.

> *MARK TAKES A BREATH.*

JENN   No kidding. How are you going to tell if you're a star-crossed lover or not?

BARBARA   I try not to be, and if I'm going to, I'd rather not know in advance. It ruins the fun.

JENN   *(To Mark.)* What do you see? Any star-crossed love affairs?

MARK   *(Looking to the sky.)* Well....

JENN   Well what?

MARK   *(With a deep breath.)* I think....

JENN   Think what?

MARK   *(With a deep breath.)* I see....

BARBARA   See what?

MARK   *(Blurting at first then falling into rhythm.)*
I think I see a tale of lovers two
who fall in love on silent starry nights
and though they knew it not, the love, at first,
they came to know it later, love, I mean.

JENN   Really?

MARK   I think I see those things in stars above....

BARBARA   *(Looking up.)* In which one do you see that?

    ENTER MIKE.

MIKE   Mark! You've got to see this! Rick's arguing with a sophomore, telling her that bell bottoms are morally wrong. "They are demonstrative of a retroactive consciousness that has no desire to grow nor advance." Come on. I think it's time for you to take him home. Oh. Am I interrupting?

MARK   Well....

MIKE   Well, come on then. "Bell bottoms, as a bad fashion article from a bankrupt decade, when revived in a more advanced decade, are wrong...." *(Leads Mark out.)*

JENN   Did you hear that?

BARBARA   Yes, and somehow I can believe he would.

JENN   No, I meant what Mark said.

BARBARA   About the stars?

JENN   Yes. It was almost poetry. Wasn't it great?

BARBARA   Sure. If you're into that thing.

JENN   Well, I am. What are you into? Brewers?

BARBARA   Are you talking about anyone in particular?

JENN   You know who I mean. Isn't he already occupied with....

BARBARA   I don't think so.

JENN   And what's so special about Mr. Todd?

BARBARA   I like a man with a plan. He knows where he's going. A man that certain about life is sure to be that certain about the woman he hangs around with.

JENN   Oh, right. And you think English majors are wishy-washy dreamy little Byrons that chase anything that moves?

BARBARA   Byron is gender exclusive. They can be Millays, too.

JENN   Oh yeah?

BARBARA   Take it easy. I'm only kidding.

JENN   You're a pragmatist.

BARBARA   You're a romantic.

JENN   You're a....

> *ENTER TODD.*

BARBARA   Hi, Todd.

TODD   Barbara. I was just looking for you.

BARBARA   You were?

TODD   I was. Tina Liscombe just told me what you said in your section of Bio lab, and I wanted to compliment you on your answer. I bet the T.A. turned green.

BARBARA   You came out here just to tell me that?

TODD   Ulterior motive. You need a drink?

BARBARA   Is that an ulterior motive too?

TODD   You bet it is.

BARBARA   You bet I do. *(Casts a meaningful glance to Jenn.)* Excuse us.

JENN   Sure.

> *EXIT BARBARA AND TODD.*

JENN   Well, at least some of us aren't alone. Where are the other lone English majors when you need them? *(Walks upstage and sits on a bench, partially obscured by foliage and darkness.)*

Scene IV

Same as before.

ENTER MARK.

MARK   She's gone. *(Paces a bit, but does not see Jenn. Looks at sky for a moment before speaking.)*
The way to woo a normal woman is
to be a normal man, or so I'd guess.
To woo a woman such as she, who's not,
well, abnormal, but yet beyond
the norm in all her virtues and the like.
So fair, as is a warming day in May,
so calm, the greenest sea beneath the sun
could do no better for seamen to weather.
Oh Eros, hear my petty little plea,
and bring her fragrant love to me!
Erato, give me words and winning songs
(Holds up hand.) to put her lovely hand where it belongs.

JENN STANDS UP.

MARK   Oh Aphrodite, dare I dream......

ENTER MIKE AND RICK—JENN IS MOTIONLESS.

MIKE   What's this? Another soliloquy?

MARK   *(Hangs head.)* Well, yeah.

MIKE   There, there, only three more semesters and you'll be out of its system.

RICK   By then it will have become a habit of the heart, in which case Mark's syntax and semantics will have been permanently......

MIKE   Quiet, Phil. I think you've said too much already.

RICK   I was only serving as the gadfly to.....

MIKE   Christ, when I say to a woman, "I like your eyes," I don't need you hovering over me asking me to define my standards in terms of aesthetic merit of ocular systems. I can't believe I invited you along.

RICK   You didn't.

MIKE   I won't make that mistake again. Come on, let's cruise. I think my chances of getting anywhere have been squelched by now.

MARK   Okay. I just need to say farewell to someone....*(Goes to patio door and looks in and sees Barbara and Todd.)* Oh. Well. A pity, that's plan B then.

MIKE   Let's begone then.

         EXEUNT MARK, MIKE, AND RICK.

JENN   *(Coming forward.)* Dare to dream.

ACT THE SECOND

Scene I

Mark's Bedroom. A bed, a dresser, a desk, a door stage right. Mark is writhing in bed.

MARK   Oh, cease, my sweet tormenting thoughts,
for ere you came, I wont to sleep at night,
except, of course, before a big exam.
But now, with dreams of Barbara Holt,
a silent siren sings me to sleep
and taunts me when I wake without her touch.
I'd rather lie awake than see the hope
in hopeless causes I might want to take.
No remedy for me there is
no oil, no salve to oint my burning heart,
except the poison that will make it worse:
your soft acetometaphinic smile,
your dancing ibuprofin eyes.
Were I a more than mortal man, I would....

     KNOCK ON DOOR.

MARK   Come in!

     ENTER MIKE.

MIKE   You didn't come down for breakfast. What's up?

MARK   I'm not feeling all too well.

MIKE   I told you that nacho dip was really Mexican.

MARK   I didn't have any of the nacho dip.

MIKE   With good Mexican food, you just need to get too close.

MARK   My head is pounding and my tongue is thick. My heart is beating much too fast for its own good, and my stomach is twisting and rolling like an unladen vessel in a tempest.

MIKE   You going to class?

MARK Of what good would a class do to one in my condition?

MIKE What good is it to burn up an absence when you're sick?

MARK I had a really strange dream last night.

MIKE Was it one where scantily clad girls chanted and danced around you and gave you things?

MARK No....

MIKE I keep trying to have a dream like that, but I never can.

MARK In my dream, I was in a garden, and I saw this really pretty white rose. It wasn't on a bush or anything, it was standing by itself, almost like a sunflower, but about two foot tall....

MIKE Aha! A phallic symbol!

MARK And when I reached to pick it, I got pricked by a thorn. I held my thumb up to look at it, and the blood dripped off my thumb and onto the flower, I guess. I looked back down at the rose, and my blood was turning it red. What do you think it means?

MIKE I think it means you should pick the mushrooms out of the salads you get here. I don't trust them myself.

MARK I'm serious.

MIKE Me, too. Hallucinogens are bad right before bed. As for a deep interpretation, you'll have to ask young Phil about it.

MARK Indeed.

MIKE I've got to go. I've got a nine o'clock, and I have to return Cortney Chestnut's notes.

MARK Isn't that your class in Victorian Lit? I thought I gave you my notebook from last year.

MIKE Yep, you did, but I like Cortney's handwriting much better. Later.

EXIT MIKE.

MARK Oh faint and dreamy flower, oh, Barbara Holt,
oh, let my arms your hortus conclusus be!
I'll hold you tight, and keep you warmly safe
from harsh impending storms and burning winds
that.....

KNOCK ON DOOR.

MARK Sheesh. Come in, Rick!

ENTER RICK.

RICK How did you know it was me?

MARK Mike just left, and the Pope isn't in America.

RICK Yes, I just saw Mike in the corridor. He said you are ill.

MARK Indeed I am.

RICK What's wrong?

MARK I don't know. It might be the flu or something. I have a
pounding head and I'm rather sick to my stomach.

RICK Could be gastroenteritis.

MARK I don't think it's that serious.

RICK An outbreak of cryptosporidiosis.

MARK No, no. Could be more serious.

RICK More serious than crypto in the water?

MARK It could be love.

RICK Oh, that.

MARK So what do your philosophers say about love?

RICK   Everything. What kind of love? Divine? Brotherly? Romantic? Appreciation of art? Sex? Ayn Rand saw sex as metaphysical. She even did an interview with *Playboy* magazine. Could you see three pictures of Plato with different facial expressions as he rapped with Hef? There's even an anthology called *Philosophy and Sex* in the bookstore. Grand document. There are defenses for adultery and case studies in promiscuity....

MARK   I meant, of course, cupiditas.

RICK   Cupiditas?

MARK   Say that there was this woman that this guy liked....

RICK   A friend, of course.

MARK   ...And he didn't know if she liked him or not, and he doesn't know whether or not he should ask her out, because he doesn't want to look stupid or anything. What would your masters say?

RICK   William James gave the parable of the mountain trail. You are walking on a mountain trail, and you come to a wide gorge. You turn back, only to discover that a ravine you passed through has become blocked by a rock slide, and you cannot climb the walls. The only way out is to jump the gorge. Or, I suppose, you could sit and starve.

MARK   Or build a signal fire and hope that park rangers would see it and send out a helicopter for you.

RICK   There's no wood, okay? Just rock. No grass, and your lighter is out of fluid. Besides, William James didn't expect the helicopter. He wasn't writing about a national park.

MARK   Okay. Sorry.

RICK   The point is that you've got to believe you can make the jump, or else you are going to fail anyway. You have to believe you can do something when you do it. The Will to Believe, it's called. You, I mean this guy, should ask her out. He should believe he can do it, because if he doesn't, he won't try and won't, whereas if he tries, he just might succeed. Besides, falling from a great height is a quicker death than starvation.

MARK   Great. Unless you just sustain internal injuries and are able to drag yourself within sight of a hospital before you die.

RICK   Isn't that a happy thought?

MARK   Indeed.

RICK   Well, fifty percent of the students in this room are planning on going to class today, in which case, I have to go. I'll drop by after my twelve o'clock to check up on you. Maybe bring you some chicken soup from the commissary.

MARK   That'll help.

RICK   See you then.

   EXIT RICK.

MARK   So thus, I must believe in Barbara Holt,
   or in myself, a harder task to take,
   And so, if I'm to win her graceful love,
   I'll have to toughen up and make a move.

Scene II

Mark's Bedroom, same as before, now around one o'clock. Mark is writing something, which he folds in thirds and puts into an envelope. He licks the envelope when there is a knock on the door.

MARK   Come in.

   ENTER RICK.

RICK   Good afternoon. Feeling better?

MARK   I daresay not. It might be a permanent ailment, something that has tainted my blood forever.

RICK   Lyme disease? I doubt it. Not too many deer ticks on campus.

   MARK LOOKS AT ENVELOPE.

RICK   Say, I took this off of a bulletin board for you. The campus theatre's doing Shakespeare's *A Midsummer Night's Dream* this weekend. I assumed you'd want to go.

MARK   Shakespeare? I'm there.

RICK   I thought so. *(Hands announcement to Mark.)*

MARK   *(Looks at envelope for a moment.)* Rick, will you do me a favor?

RICK   I could.

MARK   I'll owe you my life and all its bounty.

RICK   Yes, you will.

MARK   Can you deliver a letter for me?

RICK   Postal service will do that for a couple bits. Half as much as I'm doing it for.

MARK   Ouch. I know, but I went this sent specially.

RICK   A big red envelope, eh? Not a letter bomb now, is it?

MARK   No, but the letter may indeed bomb.

RICK   Good. I need both my hands, thank you very much.

MARK   Lucky Mike wasn't here to hear you say that.

RICK   I suppose I am. So where's it going? *(Gestures for the envelope and Mark gives it to him.)* Just the address?

MARK   Just the address. Now off with it!

RICK   Yes, sir. If it rains, sleets, or snows, you're out of luck, though.

        EXIT RICK.

MARK   So off to Reinert Hall, my hopes inside,
        to two twenty-seven, where does Miss Holt reside!

Scene III

A Campus Mall. Rick enters stage right bearing the big red envelope.

RICK I wonder what's in here. *(Looks at envelope.)* A love letter. For Reinert Hall two twenty-seven. Wait a minute. When I consulted the Student Directory this morning, it listed Jenn Walters as residing in room two twenty-two. Mark, Mark, Mark, you are such a sloppy Romeo. *(He takes a pen from his shirt pocket.)* A little loop, and *(He writes on the envelope.)* we have a little love letter to Jenn Walters. Ah, to be young and in love! Mark certainly finds her attractive as she mirrors his own values, particularly their love for English literature. They can sit over a candlelit table discussing the virtues of deconstructionism and Derrida and neo-Classicism. If only I could find someone like that. A winter night in front of a fire, debating the ethical implications of the definition of life. Slowly entangling our semantics and stripping each other of fallacies until our positions stood naked before our reason and.... *(Looks at envelope.)* Well, at least one of us can be happy here, and the other one can be a sound reasoner. *(Starts walking toward stage left but stops suddenly.)* Wait a minute. I saw *Rosencrantz and Guildenstern Are Dead. (Looks at envelope.)* Nah, Mark's uncle didn't kill his father....*(Exits stage left.)*

Scene IV

Jenn's Bedroom. Similar to Mark's but door is on opposite side. Jenn is on the telephone.

JENN Come on, it won't be that bad. It's a comedy you know. It's about lovers, and fairies, and love dust. Come on, it won't be that bad. It'll be a great chance to pick up medieval men. Oh, you know the one I mean. No, he hasn't asked me. I haven't seen him since Todd's party. I hope I do see him, though. *(The envelope, unseen by Jenn, is slipped under the door.)* I'll bet he's going. I hope I see him and can get him to ask me to go. He's strange, but not in a bad way. How? I know, he talks funny, but it's kind of cute I think. Yes, I will. You going to the club tonight? Meet me outside in about ten minutes. I have this thing to read for my Sentimental Movement class, but life's too short to spend being sentimental at twenty. See you in a bit. *(Hangs up the phone and sees the envelope. She picks it up and* *looks it over.)* What's this? Two twenty-two. That's me. *(Opens the envelope and reads.)* 'To the bearer of the chalice of my love, To she who may choose to drink of my soul and deeply imbibe of all that I am or may choose mercilessly pour my being to the ground to sate the thirsty stones, I seek to acknowledge your beauty that shines more brightly than all the stars that poets have written of for centuries. Whatever words I could ever hope to darken pages with could never hope to truly speak of the shimmering perfection that you possess. If I may be so bold and presumptuous to place these humble words into your eyes and into your heart, it would please me so to reflect as a mirror the wonder that is you. Your eyes are brilliant gems, beyond the diamond in their clarity and sharpness, beyond the ruby in their fire, beyond the sapphire in their openness. Your hair is ambrosia sweeter than the gods have ever touched; your shoulders, soft and white, are strongly set or sweetly submissive depending on your mood; your lips are petulant and playful all; your cheeks are dimpled soft when you smile and delicately drawn when you are not; oh how to go on, what words to continue that express thee true! I fail, I surrender the attempt! Mercy and pity upon the poor sojourner that pauses in reluctant awe!' A secret admirer. Where are those Philo 103 notes? *(She goes to her desk and pulls out a stapled photocopied set of notes.)* That's just what I thought. You're not so secret, Mr. Dever.

Scene V

Campus Mall outside Reinert Hall. Barbara is standing and waiting for Jenn. Todd enters and approaches Barbara. Rick, returning from his errand, passes behind them unseen and exits stage.

TODD   Hi, Barb, what's up?

BARBARA   No much. Headed off to Fallout. College night, you know.

TODD   Want someone to come along and feed you drinks?

BARBARA   Not me. Jenn might appreciate it, though.

TODD   Would you, though?

BARBARA   I might enjoy the company, I suppose.

TODD   Oh, wait. I can't. I've got an Amnesty International meeting tonight. Sorry. I'll make it up to you. The theatre department is putting on a play this weekend. Want to go?

BARBARA   I've already made plans to go with Jenn, but you're more than welcome to come along.

TODD   Oh. I'll have to pass on that one, too. Are you doing anything next Saturday night?

BARBARA   I don't think so.

TODD   I'll see if I can scare up something exciting and interesting to do. I'll give you a call tomorrow, okay?

BARBARA   I look forward to it.

TODD   See you later then. *(Exits stage right.)*

BARBARA   I look forward to it.

> ENTER MARK STAGE RIGHT—HE APPROACHES BARBARA.

MARK   Good evening, Miss Holt. How farest ye?

BARBARA   What?

MARK   Why, fairest yet upon the earth are you.
How farest ye, that fairest yet, Miss Holt?
Art thou too well, but ne'er too well, for I,
a ne'er-do-well, another Ned Kno'well,
can never know too well that you are well.

BARBARA   That was a compliment, right? Thanks. I think.

MARK   I'm sorry, Miss, I get quite taken when
I spiel like Jonson or old Shakespeare did.
I mean to say, in English of today.
What's up? And, how are you this afternoon?

BARBARA   I'm fine.

MARK   And I am better for the knowledge so.

BARBARA   And how are you this sunny afternoon?

MARK   Beyond this simple fine I am today,
   beyond the good, beyond the tritened 'okay'.
   Oh, wow, I rhymed that time. An accident.

BARBARA   Well, you're an English major. I guess you can do that
once in a while.

MARK   I guess I can, and sometimes guess I do,
   but since I'm here and speaking English stuff with you,
   the thespians on campus stage will play
   the fairies and the Greeks as Shakespeare wrought
   and wrote about in comic Junish dreams.
   Will you accompany this fool to it?

BARBARA   You rhymed again.

MARK   I am an English major through, my lass.

BARBARA   I thought lass was a Scottish word.

MARK   No matter, yet my matter stands in wait.
   Care you to see the play with humble me?

BARBARA   I'd really like to, but I have other plans for Saturday night.
   Sorry.

> *ENTER JENN FROM BACK STAGE, UNSEEN. SHE IS
> CARRYING THE RED ENVELOPE, BUT WHEN SHE SEES
> MARK, SHE STUFFS IT UNDER HER SHIRT.*

MARK   Not quite as sorry as am I, Miss Holt,
   and I shall take my leave of you. Good night.

JENN   *(Coming forward.)* Hi, Mark.

MARK   Hello, Jenn.

JENN   What's up?

MARK   Not much.

JENN   Where you headed?

MARK   Over to Mike's.

JENN   Want to go to Fallout with us?

MARK   No thank 'ee.

JENN   Come on. I need someone to dance with.

MARK   I never dance in public. People think I'm having a seizure.

JENN   Oh. Did you hear about the play this weekend?

MARK   Indeed. I could not miss Shakespeare.

JENN   Are you going?

MARK   I've thought about it.

JENN   Me, too. Have you ever seen *A Midsummer Night's Dream* produced?

MARK   Once. A professional group. I wonder how the students will do. I guess we'll see Saturday.

JENN   Yeah, I guess so.

MARK   Well, I better get over to Mike's. Fare thee well, ladies.

JENN   Bye, Mark.

BARBARA   See you.

> *EXIT MARK STAGE LEFT.*

JENN   He's so shy.

BARBARA   I don't know about that.

JENN   *(Pulls out red envelope.)* Look what he sent me. *(Gives the envelope to Barbara.)*

BARBARA   *(Reads a bit.)* He sure is a strange one.

JENN   He sent it anonymous. Kind of romantic, don't you think?

BARBARA   I suppose. *(Hands envelope back to Jenn.)*

JENN   I wish he would have asked me to the play. *(Puts envelope in her purse.)*

BARBARA   Me, too. You know who just asked me to the play?

JENN   Who?

BARBARA   Todd Russell.

JENN   Are you going with him?

BARBARA   No, I'm going with you.

JENN   You're crazy. You should have, You've got the hots for him so bad you set off the fire alarms twice last week.

BARBARA   That was a prankster, not me.

JENN   Oh, but you do.

BARBARA   He is rather handsome.

JENN   And he's rich.

BARBARA   And he knows what he's going to do with his life. A lot of guys here don't.

JENN   And he's rich.

BARBARA   And he's rich.

JENN   I knew it! You're a gold-digger!

BARBARA   Might as well dig for something precious.

JENN   Right on! Let's go dig for some drinks!

    EXEUNT.

Scene VI

Campus Mall. Same as before, except empty. Mark and Mike enter, walking. Mike stops.

MIKE   She lives up there, you know.

MARK   *(In a low voice.)* Who do you mean?

MIKE   Why, Jenn, of course. Who else would I mean, Mr. Dever?

MARK   *(Looks down.)* I didn't know. That's why I asked.

MIKE   Come now, when you lie, you MUST keep the eye contact. Otherwise I would know that you were afraid I was going to say Barbara Holt.

MARK   Barbara Holt?

MIKE   Next tip: Don't repeat the last thing the accuser says. So'd you ask her out yet?

MARK   Ask her out?

MIKE   What am I, a narcissist? Never mind. 'Yes, Mike, I asked her out.'

MARK   Yes, Mike, I asked her out.

MIKE   'Yes, Mike, I asked Barbara Holt out'?

MARK   Yes, Mike, I asked Barbara Holt out.

MIKE   'And I'll be a sonova gun, Mike, but she said "Yes," and then we exchanged rings and bodily fluids, not necessarily in that order'?

MARK   Didn't go quite so well as that.

MIKE   No ring?

MARK   No.

MIKE   No bodily fluids?

MARK   No.

MIKE   Good thinking. The bodily fluids tend to get you into one form of trouble or another.

MARK   No date.

MIKE   No date? Why not? You didn't....

MARK HANGS HEAD.

MIKE   Not the iambic pentameter. You asked her to the Shakespeare play, didn't you? You talked like a Renaissance dork again, didn't you?

MARK   Well.....

MIKE   I keep telling you, you've got to talk like you were born in this century. Be yourself. Don't be some cheap Astrophel knockoff.

MARK   What if I am a cheap Astrophel knock-off?

MIKE   Then pretend to be a cheap knock-off of me. Just be cool, be natural when you ask a woman out.

MARK   I'd rather stick with the Spenser imitation.

MIKE   Look, you have to be normal when you approach women....

MARK   Normal? Normal? What is normal? Getting married to someone you end up divorcing later, or better yet, someone you end up hating but won't get divorced because of the kids, and arguing endlessly about money and not being able to have any more children and then blowing your freaking brains out while your kid's at his grandmother's house in Ava?

MIKE   That's not normal either.

MARK   Well, what is?

MIKE   Normal is what it's not. Normal's not spitting Shakespeare. Try this one: "Hey, Barbara, what's up?"

MARK   Hey Barbara Holt, what's up this fine spring day?

MIKE   "Hey, Barbara, what's up?"

MARK   *(Sighs and slowly, with effort.)* Hey, Barbara Holt, what's new this afternoon?

MIKE   *(Shakes his head.)* Better. Now try this one: So how was your one o'clock?

MARK   How fared ye in your one o'clock today?

MIKE   We'll work on it.

    EXEUNT.

ACT THE THIRD

Scene I

College Mall Barbara and Jenn are walking across the stage. Enter Todd with Penny, both dressed elegantly.

JENN Uh oh, look who it is.

BARBARA It's Todd Russell.

JENN Who's that?

BARBARA Who cares?

JENN Hey, now....

> *TODD AND PENNY APPROACH.*

TODD Hi, Jenn. Hi, Barbara. Are you guys ready for the play?

JENN How ready do we need to be?

TODD It's in old English, you know.

JENN It's in Middle English, if you must know. Or is post-modern English all they teach you in Mass Comm?

TODD Post-modern English? Is that what we speak?

PENNY Hi, my name is Penny.

JENN That's nice.

BARBARA Jenn.... My name is Barbara.

PENNY How do you do?

BARBARA Well enough. You?

PENNY Better than some, not so good as others.

TODD   Good to see you ladies. We're going to go in to get good seats.

BARBARA Enjoy the play.

TODD   See you later.

PENNY Thank you. Nice meeting you.

> *EXEUNT TODD AND PENNY.*

JENN   The nerve of that guy!

BARBARA Easy, Jenn.

JENN   He asked you out and then came with someone else!

BARBARA I said no. It's his right.

JENN   But it's not right. Do you think she meant anyone in particular by 'better than some'?

BARBARA I could care less.

JENN   I'll bet you could. But could you care more? And he had to come right up to us and start talking.

BARBARA You'd rather have him slink in and out like he was doing something wrong?

JENN   I don't know. I think so.

> *ENTER MARK.*

BARBARA Calm down. Here comes your man.

> *MARK APPROACHES.*

JENN   Hi, Mark. Are you ready for the play?

MARK   Indeed, as ready as a man could ever be.

JENN   Where's Mike?

MARK   He has to study for a Victorian Lit exam.

JENN   Rick?

MARK   Rick's not much into Shakespeare. I don't know if I'd bring
him to something I wanted to enjoy aesthetically anyway. He'd turn
A Midsummer Night's Dream into a free will versus determinism debate.

JENN   I bet he would.

BARBARA So you came alone?

MARK   Indeed, for when the choice lies there between
to have that which I want and nothing else,
there lies no choice at all for me to make.

JENN   You just need to learn to ask for what you want. Ask the right
way, and anything can be yours.

MARK   Then I shall try to learn the right way to ask.

JENN   You probably know the right way, you just haven't tried.

BARBARA You never can tell. Your asking might need some polish,
too.

JENN   But not too much. There's something to be said for youthful
innocence and exuberance.

MARK   Thank you, your thoughts will help me in my quest.
And now, onto the words that Shakespeare wrought.
(Moves to exit.)

JENN   Would you like to sit with us, Mark?

MARK   I think I'll not, my dearest Jenn, but thanks. *(Exit.)*

JENN   I wonder why he doesn't just ask me out. It must have been
you.

BARBARA Me?

JENN   He probably couldn't ask me out because you were there. Like
at the party. He couldn't ask me out because you were there. That's
why he sent the letter. He's trying to tell me, but he's afraid of what
would happen if I said no. He'd be crushed and even worse if
someone else saw it. I just need to get him alone.

BARBARA You sure that's it?

JENN   What else could it be? I'll catch him when he comes out of the play. I'll ask him to come to the Fall Frolic. Can you disappear for a while? We can still go to The Rage afterwards.

BARBARA   That's okay. We don't have to go to the bar.

JENN   No, really, I don't mind. Unless Mark wants to go out. I tell you what, how about you wait for me in front of Reinert, and if I'm not there at seven o'clock, I'm out with Mark.

BARBARA   Oh, sure, I'll just stand in front of the dorm for an hour waiting for you.

JENN   Well, it might take a while. You know how Mark is and how he talks. It might take him two minutes to poem out a yes.

BARBARA   Fine. Are you ready to see the play now?

JENN   Let's.

   EXEUNT.

Scene II

Campus Mall, same as before. Jenn and Barbara are crossing downstage, and they pause in the center of downstage.

JENN   I loved that! I wish I had a jar of fairy dust. Just think of all the men I could get to fall in love with me.

BARBARA   I thought you wanted just one.

JENN   Oh, I do, but it would be neat to have all the men on campus in love with me. I'd never have to buy a drink again.

   TODD AND PENNY, ENMESHED IN A CONVERSATION, CROSS UPSTAGE RIGHT TO LEFT.

BARBARA   *(Looking off stage left.)* Sounds like Heaven.

JENN   *(Looking off stage right.)* Here comes my Hero. Barb, please.....

BARBARA   All right, all right, I'm gone. *(Exits stage left.)*

ENTER MARK STAGE RIGHT.

JENN   Mark! What's up?

MARK   Good production, don't you think?

JENN   I liked it. Hang on. *(Mimes grabbing a handful of dust from her bag and blows it in Mark's direction.)* Say, you know that there's going to be the Fall Frolic Festival tomorrow.

MARK   The Fall Frolic Festival.

JENN   I know, I know, but they got the alliteration, didn't they?

MARK   Actually, I did know about it. I just like saying it. Makes me sound like Sylvester the cat.

JENN   I was thinking about going.

MARK   It should be fun.

JENN   I really hadn't decided though.

MARK   The Macgraw Machine is going to be playing. I like them, even if they did that song "Little Hamlet."

JENN   Mark, would you like to go to the festival with me?

MARK   Mike, Rick, and I were planning on going together. I suppose you can come along.

JENN   I meant you and me.

MARK   I already promised to go with them.

JENN   Oh, all right. Some other time maybe then.

MARK   I don't know. We'll see. I have to get going.

JENN   Right. See you later.

MARK   Fare thee well. *(Exits.)*

JENN   What's the deal, Mark? *(Wanders upstage.)*

ENTER RICK.

RICK   *(Not seeing Jenn.)* Ah, to be young and in love. His very perceptions must be altered by his state of affections. *(Picks a flower.)* This very bloom, or one similar, will seem tantalizing in its scent and sight, a very metaphor for his beloved. A Heliopsis helianthoides, I believe. He will take it thus *(Holds near end of stem and sniffs before extending it to an imaginary lover.)* and say something English major and romantic. "Oh, idealistically compatible soul, I value your existence as much as my own and find your company fulfilling and compelling to compare...." *(Sees Jenn.)* Er....

JENN   Hi, Rick, right?

RICK   Hello.

JENN   Who were you talking about just now?

RICK   When?

JENN   Just now.

RICK   What did I say?

JENN   Something about an English major being in love.

RICK   Are you sure?

JENN   Positive. Who were you talking about?

RICK   Sometimes the acoustical layout of campus malls leads one to the impression that someone nearby was speaking of an English major when in fact that someone might have been speaking merely of hypothetical English majors.

JENN   Were you talking about Mark?

RICK   Mark? No!

JENN   Are you sure?

RICK   Absolutely certain. Well, as certain as one can be. I believe I am certain, but of course nothing is absolute. We are only sure until we are called into Doubt, and then we can restore Belief only through the process of inquiry, which Charles Sanders Peirce dealt with in his essay "The Fixation of Belief." He was the forerunner of Pragmatism, you know, before William.....

JENN Who were you talking about, then?

RICK William James? The founder of the Pragmatic philosophy along with Charles Sanders Peirce and the author of....

JENN I meant the English major.

RICK What English major?

JENN The one you were talking about.

RICK When?

JENN Who was the English major you were talking about when you saw me?

RICK Mike! It was Mike.

JENN Mike's not an English major.

RICK He was.

JENN When?

RICK Sometime between Anthropology and Spanish, I think.

JENN And who's Mike in love with?

RICK Can't tell you.

JENN Why not?

RICK I can't.

JENN Okay. You're not a good liar, you know.

RICK I wouldn't be. I don't practice much.

JENN You're both crazy!

RICK Hardly certifiable, but we do have our quirks.

JENN I can't even talk to you!

RICK Why not?

JENN   Argh! *(Wanders back upstage.)*

RICK SHRUGS AND EXITS STAGE LEFT.

ENTER MIKE STAGE RIGHT.

MIKE   Sigh, Chestnut hair, Cortney, love. I could gaze at her forever.

JENN   *(Turning.)* Courtly love?

MIKE   Oh, hi, there. How are you doing?

JENN   I don't know. What's the story with Mark? Is he shy or what?

MIKE   Mark? Shy? A little I guess. No more than most English majors.

JENN   Oh, hardly.

MIKE   Right. Sorry.

JENN   You said Mark didn't have a girlfriend. Why not?

MIKE   He likes being single. He's going to be a bachelor for life. I, on the other hand....

JENN   He ever go out with women?

MIKE   Oh, sure. He did have a steady for a while his freshman year. Got heartbroken though and gave up, whereas I always bounce back.

JENN   Oh, what happened?

MIKE   Oh, between Mark and Cathy? It's a long story. Say, if you have the time, I'd be glad to tell you. You want to move this to Duffy's? It's kind of chilly out here, and I could use a beer.....

MIKE LEADS JENN OFF STAGE RIGHT.

Scene III

Outside Reinert Hall, seven p.m.

> *ENTER MARK. HE LOOKS AT THE HALL FOR A FEW*
> *MINUTES AND PACES ABOUT.*

MARK   So there she lives in Reinert's hallowed hall,
upon the second floor, so far away
and fourteen windows from the right
(unless the numbers start some other way).
What do you now, my sweetest Barbara Holt?
Lie you awake amid some swirling dream
of poets penning scores of hearty work?
What fills your mind this autumn night, my dear?
The images of a you and me entangled in
a tight and snuggly warm embrace
beneath the winking stars of fading skies
upon the blanket of the fallen leaves?
Oh, Barbara Holt, were that you were right here,
I'd seize the waning day and seize your hand
and.....

> *ENTER BARBARA FROM STAGE LEFT.*

BARBARA   And no call, as if I'm going to be waiting by the phone. Probably forgot anyway. And then it's go and wait for your best friend.... *(Sees Mark.)* Oh, hi, Mark.

MARK   Good den, Miss Holt. Your grace denies the stars
their share of Heaven; they hate you for the deed.

BARBARA   Oh. Thank you. I think.

MARK   No thanks are needed for the spoken truth.

BARBARA   Are you looking for Jenn?

MARK   No, Jenn holds not my throbbing heart in hand.

BARBARA   She was looking for you earlier.

MARK   Indeed, I met Miss Walters on the mall.

BARBARA So are you going to Fall Frolic with her?

MARK   She'll frolic on without my company,
for I had plans to go with Mike and Rick.
Oh, zounds, where is my petty poet mind?
I could have rhymed with frolic and with Rick....

BARBARA No need to strain yourself for me.

MARK   No strain for me, Miss Barbara Holt, to rhyme.
Heck, I can rhyme at almost any time.
Besides, and even if it was a strain,
no better gain for the semantic pain.

BARBARA I see. She really likes you, you know. She's always talking about you.

MARK   And you, sweet Barbara Holt, what thinkest you?

BARBARA I think you and she would make a cute couple.

MARK   Oh ho! How soon I forgot my vow! *(Seizes her hand.)*
I meant, Miss Holt, what think you of an us,
a we between a me and a gentle you?
I'd pluck the twinkling stars from quiet skies
to just compare them with your dancing eyes
to only cast them down when they've lost the test?
Oh can't you see us in a grassy field,
with a basket of food, perhaps some wine,
to idle hours in warm sunlight, just us?
Oh say you do, and say you will, we might?
That's all I softly ask of you tonight.

BARBARA Well....

MARK   Indeed, I think it all is well. Do you?

BARBARA Look, Mark, Jenn really likes you. She would never forgive me if I....well, you know. Besides, I'm not really into English majors. You know.

MARK   Indeed, I fear I do know what you mean.

BARBARA You say you saw Jenn?

MARK NODS.

BARBARA Well, it's seven o'clock. Just like her. Well, I'll see you. I have this biology homework I want to recopy for class Monday.

MARK Good night, Miss Holt, and dream a possible dream.

BARBARA You too. *(Exits.)*

MARK I never dream an impossible dream, Miss Holt,
but sometimes think I do; and so our love,
or maybe just love-liking, is not so;
impossible, I mean, we can yet be.
It is a lucky thing that I'm a fool.
Another man would've quit by now, but I,
the unrequited unrequitting lover kind,
have sparked a sudden plan to win
your favor, dearest Barbara Holt. Watch out.

ACT THE FOURTH

Scene I

Mark's Bedroom, nine a.m. Sunday morning. Mark pulls a big red sheet of paper out of his typewriter and reads over it. He nods and there is a knock at the door.

MARK Come on in, Rick.

ENTER RICK.

RICK You rang?

MARK *(Putting the sheet of paper into the big red envelope.)* I have another favor to ask.

RICK I already have your life and all its bounty. What do you have to offer? Your firstborn?

MARK How about my Spin Doctors CD collection?

RICK *(Shaking head.)* Please.

MARK A six pack of Rolling Rock?

RICK Inconceivable.

MARK I give up. What do you want?

RICK Think of something you could offer me that would make me do it.

MARK How about the thrill of doing something for a friend?

RICK The pleasure of assisting a friend in pursuit of something we both value. Perhaps I will learn something useful in the process, and of course, the experience.

MARK You mean I could have gotten off this easily the first time?

RICK Yes.

MARK Can I have my life and all its bounty back?

RICK   Sorry, no refunds nor exchanges. *(Takes letter.)* Another large red envelope.

MARK   Yes. Off with it.

RICK   *(Looking at envelope.)* At least you got the address right this time. *(Exits.)*

MARK   Got the right address this time? *(Shrugs, begins to walk, but stops.)* I forgot to sign it with Mike's name. Well, it will all be revealed at some time. I just hope Barbara didn't show her the first one. Ah, well....

>   *MIKE BURSTS THROUGH THE DOOR.*

MIKE   You slime!

MARK   What?

MIKE   Are you attracted to Jenn Walters?

MARK   Not really.

MIKE   She sure thinks you have it for her pretty bad. Cripes, you're all she could talk about last night at Duffy's. Mark this and Mark that. What's your secret? I could use it.

MARK   I don't know.

MIKE   Well, that's all right. You're forgiven. So how's Barbara Holt?

MARK   She's fine.

MIKE   I know. How is she? Oh, you meant she is fine fine. Right. You ask her out again?

MARK   Sort of.

MIKE   I don't like the sound of that. What did you say?

MARK   I asked her to go out.

MIKE   Okay, okay, how did you ask her out?

MARK   I asked her if she wanted to go have a picnic.

MIKE   Blank verse?

MARK   Well....

MIKE   Damn it, cut that out! You'll never get a date with her if you do that.

MARK   How do you know?

MIKE   I know. Okay, you want go out with Barbara Holt?

MARK   Come on.

MIKE   Yes or no?

MARK   Indeed, I'd give my life to date Miss Holt.

MIKE   *(Counting syllables on fingers.)* 'Indeed, I'd give my life to date Miss Holt.' All I have to do is mention her name. Do you realize what a putz it makes you look like?

MARK   I care not if I seem a putz to you.

MIKE   Stop it! Stop it!

MARK   Stop what, my freaked-out friend? The way I talk?

MIKE   Yes. Come on, you don't talk like that around me and Rick. You're going to look like you're putting on airs. Barbara Holt is going to think you're just some goofball English major.

MARK   'Slid! Indeed she does! *(Pauses.)* I mean, yeah.

MIKE   If she just sees you as this blank-verse spouting English major, she'll not see your good points.

MARK   That's right. I'm not only an English major, I'm a Renaissance man.

MIKE   Let's leave the Renaissance out of this for now. Okay. So what are your good points?

    MARK SHRUGS.

MIKE   Well, you have excellent taste in friends, and good enough taste in women.

MARK   Mmm-hmm.

MIKE   All right, you're honest, sincere, and naive. Good points. Well, sort of.

MARK   Mmm-hmmm.

MIKE   So we'll just have to play these up. Somehow.

Scene II

Campus Mall. Rick crosses the back of stage bearing the red envelope. Enter Todd with Penny.

PENNY Don't even bring up the f-words again.

TODD   Come on, Penny. There'll be music, and dancing, and free food.

PENNY I wanted to spend some time with you in front of your fireplace. Maybe cook you a couple pancakes.

TODD   Pancakes?

PENNY It's all I know how to cook.

TODD   We can go for dinner to Cincerelli's and then to the Fall Frolic Festival. Come on, Penny.

PENNY You just don't understand, do you? *(Exits stage right.)*

TODD   I guess not.

     ENTER JENN AND BARBARA STAGE LEFT.

JENN   So we should just....*(Sees Todd.)* Well, I have to run, I'll see you later. Hi, Todd.

TODD   Hello, ladies.

BARBARA Give me a call, Jenn.

EXIT JENN STAGE RIGHT.

BARBARA What's up, Todd?

TODD What are you doing this afternoon, dear Barbara?

BARBARA Well, Jenn and I were planning on going to the Fall Frolic Festival.

TODD Would you like to come with me?

BARBARA But Jenn....Yes, I would love to.

TODD Great! You want to meet there at three o'clock?

BARBARA Yes, that would be great.

TODD All right. I'll see you then. *(Exits.)*

BARBARA You better believe it.

> *RICK, RUNNING AT A FULL SPEED, ENTERS STAGE RIGHT AND ALMOST RUNS INTO BARBARA. HE STOPS WHEN HE SEES HER AND THEY PAUSE. HE STEPS LEFT AND SHE STEPS RIGHT—THEY PAUSE AGAIN. HE STEPS RIGHT AND SHE STEPS LEFT AND THEY PAUSE AGAIN. RICK TURNS TO FLEE AND EXIT STAGE RIGHT. JENN RUNS ONTO STAGE FROM STAGE RIGHT WAVING ANOTHER RED ENVELOPE. RICK AND JENN STOP FACE TO FACE. THEY PAUSE FOR A MOMENT, BUT RICK TURNS AND RUNS PAST BARBARA AND EXITS STAGE LEFT.*

JENN Come back here!

BARBARA What's that, another love letter?

JENN   Probably. *(Opens letter and reads.)* 'Jenn, sweet light of infinite skies, I bear you tidings of love from across the greatest sea of my soul. If cowards die a thousand deaths, that many would I die to merely touch your face; but yet I die within without the touch. With hair the color of chestnuts and cheeks the tint of intimate fires, how can I think of anything but being alone with you. I pray, someday, these simple subtle dreams will come true.' This one is typed, though, as if he could hide it now. Wait a minute....chestnut hair....

BARBARA What?

JENN   It's....nothing.

BARBARA Say, Jenn, Todd just came and asked me if I would go to the festival with him. I said yes.

JENN   Who am I supposed to go with then?

BARBARA I don't know. Who says you have to go with anyone? You can go by yourself if you want. Well, I have to go get ready. I'm supposed to meet him at the festival at three o'clock.

JENN   Fine.

BARBARA See you there. *(Exits.)*

JENN   See you there. *(Starts to leave stage but bumps into Penny, entering stage.)*

PENNY Excuse me. Have you seen Todd Russell?

JENN   Todd?

PENNY He and I had a disagreement, and I wanted to tell him everything is okay.

JENN   Oh. I haven't seen him.

PENNY I'll see him later at the festival then.

EXIT PENNY AND JENN ON OPPOSITE SIDES.

ACT THE FIFTH

Scene I

Fall Frolic Festival, outside. Todd stands waiting, and Jenn and Barbara enter.

TODD   Hello, ladies.

JENN   Good afternoon, Todd.

BARBARA Hi, Todd.

JENN   A Penny on your thoughts, Todd?

TODD   What?

BARBARA I'm thinking it's time to find the band.

JENN   Right. Disappearing.... *(Exit Jenn.)*

TODD   Allow me to say you look ravishing in denim.

BARBARA Go right ahead.

TODD   You look ravishing in denim.

BARBARA Thank you.

TODD   Do you like Macgraw Machine? They're playing over in the main tent.

BARBARA Let us then.

> *EXEUNT STAGE LEFT. ENTER MARK, MIKE, AND RICK STAGE RIGHT.*

MIKE   I still say we should have brought the duct tape.

RICK   Some people fear the truth when it is spoken.

MIKE   I don't fear the truth. I fear you speaking.

MARK   Come on, gents, we shall not accomplish any of our goals if we bicker.

RICK   Primary objective: to enjoy ourselves. Secondary objectives: meet compatible members of the opposite sex and to dance, eat, and drink ourselves into a Dionyistic frenzy.

MIKE   Should we synchronize watches? Come on, gentlemen, let's go!

THE THREE START TO EXIT STAGE LEFT. ENTER PENNY STAGE RIGHT.

PENNY Hey! Have you guys seen Todd?

MARK   No, dear Penny, we have just arrived.

PENNY Oh, well, if you see him, don't tell him I am looking for him. I want to surprise him. I'll show him I can be flexible and social, too, and do what he wants sometimes. *(Exits stage left.)*

MIKE   Right. What a loving, understanding, mature woman. Wasn't she on *Little House On the Prairie?*

RICK   Ad hominem. To what deep urge and subconscious motivation do we owe this attack?

MIKE   Women like that just want to hang out in the home with their man and cook dinner and sit in front of a fire. And do nothing.

MARK   Except enjoy each other's company.

MIKE   Right. Let's find that main tent. *(Sings.)* 'Little Ham, Little Ham, you're the Danish Man, who quite happily, cut down your family tree....'

MARK GRIMACES, AND AS MIKE BEGINS TO LEAD THEM OUT, MARK BUMPS INTO MIKE AND PUTS A RED ENVELOPE IN HIS BACK POCKET. RICK NOTICES AND RAISES AN EYEBROW BUT REMAINS SILENT AS THE THREE EXEUNT.

Scene II

Outside Main Tent. Barbara and Todd are walking together.

TODD   They are a bit on the goofy side, but they lay down a good bass line.

BARBARA   I suppose, if you are into bass lines. I prefer a good piano solo myself.

TODD   Listen, do you dance?

BARBARA   On occasion.

TODD   Great! Let's.....

>   *ENTER PENNY.*

PENNY Todd! I found you. I decided to come after all.

TODD   Penny! You're here.

BARBARA   I'm here, too.

PENNY Oh. Did you bring Barbara?

TODD   Oh, no, Barbara are just here as friends, you know. I just met her here, I didn't bring her or anything, it's just that I needed someone to dance with, and I'm sure you'd be more comfortable with me dancing with a friend than with a strange woman who might get the wrong idea.

BARBARA   Hard to imagine that.

PENNY You can dance with me now. Thank you, Barb.

BARBARA   It was no problem. Any decent woman would take care to make sure that Todd was not in free circulation. It's best that you keep him. Good day, Todd. Have a nice time. *(Exits.)*

PENNY I told you she had designs on you.

TODD   It's a good thing you showed when you did.

PENNY Oh, there's no need to worry. I trust you.

TODD Let's dance.

EXEUNT.

Scene III

An empty mall in the Fall Frolic Festival. Mark and Mike enter.

MIKE We did not ditch him. When Phil is done in the restroom, he'll find us.

MARK Right.

MIKE Besides, it's much quieter without him. Now I can hear myself think. "Mike, you want to meet a beautiful woman and live happily ever after, at least for a couple of weeks. Mike, you could use a beer. Mike, what did Mark stick in your back pocket? He is no master of deception." *(Reaches around and pulls big red envelope out of his back pocket.)* Good thing you are going to college, you waif, you'd never make it on the streets. *(Reads front.)* "Dear Sweet Jenn." Do I look like Jenn? *(Begins to open it.)*

MARK Don't open that!

MIKE Why not?

MARK We might run into Jenn....

> *ENTER JENN. MIKE STUFFS ENVELOPE INTO HIS BACK POCKET AGAIN.*

JENN Hi, Mark.

MIKE My dear, sweet Jenn! How are you this afternoon?

MARK Hi, Jenn.

JENN I am doing okay, I suppose. A little lonely, though. I could use some company.

MIKE   I could use some company, too. Maybe IBM, or something blue chip.

JENN   Barbara came with Todd, and I'm here all alone.

MIKE   Could be worse. You could be stuck with Phil.

MARK   Barbara came with Todd?

JENN   And I don't have anyone to dance with at the main tent. You want to come dance?

MARK   Dance?

MIKE   I'd be glad to.

JENN   Come on, Mark. You don't have to be embarrassed. I know you sent the letters. You don't have to be shy or flaky or anything. I think it's neat that you sent them, and that you talk in blank verse once in a while.

MARK   I sent the letters?

JENN   The ones in the big red envelopes.

MIKE   The letters in the big red envelopes?

JENN   I caught Rick delivering one, and he didn't say they came from you. I think he tried telling me that Mike sent them.

MIKE   Mike sent them! I mean, I sent them. Here, I have one for you now, in fact. *(Reaches into back pocket, gets down on one knee, and presents it to Jenn, head bowed.)* For you, mistress.

JENN   *(Takes letter, opens it, and reads.)* 'Dearest Jenn of the twinkling eyes, I bring to you a bouquet of words to clutch to your sighing breast on cloudy days. Were words like flowers that never fade, as beautiful as you and scented as the pale blue cloud of your aura. But words can never seem so bold upon a shelf nor thorny in your hand; words are only lovely in your heart, and I, a pale rose, am so. My humblest love and wishes, Mike Quince.'

MIKE   And I mean every word of it.

JENN   Why was the first letter in Mark's handwriting then?

MARK   First letter?

JENN   The one where you said my eyes were better than diamonds and sapphires and stuff.

> *MARK LOOKS DISTRESSED.*

MIKE   I confess I had Mark help me with the first one, because I didn't know much about love letters, and I was in such a hurry, I didn't get to type it. It was a fit of passion, you understand. I apologize. Your beauty overwhelmed me. I would say it won't happen again, but you are still beautiful.

JENN   Get up, you goof.

> *MIKE STANDS.*

JENN   So you sent me the letters. I kind of suspected when you said chestnut hair in the second one. You were working on it when I bumped into you on the mall. Why didn't you say anything then?

MIKE   *(Slipping an arm around Jenn and beginning to lead her off stage.)* Well, these things take time to do them right.

JENN   Can you talk blank verse?

MIKE   Anything for you, my dear.
I think that you are quite the best I've seen
in women here on campus malls *(Pause.)* and stuff.
Your eyes are like, are like, are like the sea
whenever it, the sea I mean, is calm.
They're blue, and they're like two deep pools.....

> *EXIT MIKE AND JENN. MARK BEGINS PACING THE EMPTY STAGE, STOPS, AND SHRUGS.*

Scene IV

Same as before: Mark is alone on the stage. He walks around a bit, and stops to pick a flower.

MARK   And what becomes of Mark N. Dever then?
Alone upon the stage of life and love,
with only dreams and....

Stop it, stop it, stop it! Funny thing, the one I love does not like the way I talk, and the one who loves the way I talk is not my love. And all I do is wander around spouting blank verse. (*He holds the flower for inspection.*)

> *ENTER BARBARA, FUMING. SHE STOPS WHEN SHE SEES MARK, AND HE CONTINUES WITHOUT SEEING HER.*

MARK   You dainty bloom, you dare compare yourself to she?
Your purple suits you well, my little friend,
highlighting each smooth curve, soft line, and bend
and tinting out your shade quite royally.
Her colors complement her much that way:
upon her cheeks, the pink carnation's blush,
upon her lips, the thornless rose's flush,
and in her eyes, a mourning glories' bouquet.
Her kiss tastes like a honeysuckle sweet.
Her hair smells of the lilac's summer air.
Her skin is tulip petal tender, yet....

(*Stops.*) Bah, what am I doing? She doesn't want to hear sonnets. Heaven knows if she even wants to hear anything I say. Oh, what's the point anyway? (*Turns to find Barbara.*) Er. Hello.

BARBARA Hi.

MARK   (*Looks again at flower and then at Barbara.*) Oh. This is a lovely flower, but I do not think it has ever seen the likes of you. (*He offers the flower to Barbara and she takes it. He studies her face for a moment.*) Is something wrong?

BARBARA Not really. Just the usual star-crossed lovers thing, except no love and no deaths at the end.

MARK   Well, I'm glad to hear that at least. Are you okay?

BARBARA I guess.

MARK   You want to go somewhere and talk about it? I am good at star-crossed lovers....

BARBARA Sure, let us.

MARK   Good day it is, Miss Barbara Holt, for me
to take you to a place I know, a....

I mean, we can go to Forest Park. There's a little lake there with a bunch of benches and....

BARBARA *(Holds flower to her face.)* So it does not compare?

MARK   Not a whit.

BARBARA Your blankened verse I deem okay, Sir Mark,
as long as it is what you really do.
Don't be something you're not.

MARK   Really?

BARBARA I've had too much of that lately. Poetry away.

MARK   A finer day it is, my Barbara Holt,
And so my chase has ended quite happily.
Were this a play, and this the final act,
the audience would see a marriage pact
to forever enjoin both you and me.

BARBARA Whoa, easy there. It might only be the third act of a tragedy.
Let's go look at your lake first and we'll take it from there.

MARK   Let us! *(He takes Barbara by the hand and leads her off stage quickly.)*

ENTER RICK FROM THE OPPOSITE.

RICK   That's no way to win Jenn, you lummock. I guess we shall have to think of something else to help you out.... *(Strokes chin and lights fall.)*

The End

Dennis Thompson

Goes On Strike

A One Act Drama

Dennis Thompson Goes On Strike

Cast of Characters

Dennis Thompson   A young man who thinks his life is the plot of a droll modern novel.

Lisa   An attractive young woman moving into an apartment across the hall from Dennis.

Chris   A longtime friend of Dennis who takes life less seriously than his bookish friend.

Scene: Dennis's Apartment.

DENNIS   *(Addressing audience.)* Oh, I know you're out there, and I know what you're doing, and I'm getting pretty sick of it. How would you like to be the pawn of forces greater than you and put on display for anyone to see? I don't think you'd care for it any more than I do. To have your moves written out and not be able to look face to face with the guy writing your life out. *(Paces.)* That does it. I've had enough of this. I'm going to mess you up. Check this out. Dennis Thompson, age 21, brown hair, blue eyes, five eleven and three quarters, one sixty, born and raised in Milwaukee, Wisconsin, 53209. Currently living alone in a rather shabby apartment on the East Side, nothing as fashionable as West Allis, but for a guy with a high school education and a job in a mail room for Northwestern Mutual, it's all I could get. There, you moron. That's exposition, and you're not allowed to do that. It felt good to muck up your story like that. *(Thinks.)* It felt so good, in fact, that I think I'm going to do more. As of right now, I am on strike. Do you hear me? You might as well put the pen down, sport, 'cause I'm done being your pawn. And the rest of you might as well put the book down 'cause it's going to get even more droll from this point on then it has been for the last hundred or thousand pages. *(Sits for a few minutes.)* How do you like not having anyone to push around? Not very much fun, eh? *(Sits for another moment.)* Well, If I'm on strike, I guess I should not go to work today, eh? *(He goes to the phone and dials.)* Mr. Barrett? It's Dennis. I don't feel very well today. I think I'm going to have to stay home. No, nothing too bad. I'll try. See you, then. *(Hangs up.)* Well, that was easy. Maybe too easy.... *(Sits back down and thinks for a while—then a knock at the door.)* And who might that be? Did you send my mother over her to tell me that I have to behave? Maybe a representative from the Fictional Characters' Local 301? *(Knock again.)* It's open!

   ENTER LISA.

LISA   Hi, my name is Lisa. Can I use your phone?

DENNIS   *(Stands and shrugs.)* It's right there.

LISA   Thanks. They haven't hooked mine up yet. I just moved in across the hall. We're neighbors. *(Begins dialing.)*

DENNIS *(Addressing stage right.)* Oh, sure, I get it. This is the love interest thing. She's a blonde, alright, but the eyes not blue, and it doesn't fall in a loose wave about her shoulders. Good looking, but not perfect. It adds a touch of realism to the story.

LISA Okay, I'll be home then. *(Hangs up.)* Moving is sure a pain in the butt. I have to wait around for the phone man, wait around for the Sears refrigerator, sit at home and wait for just about everything. Good thing I'm a pack rat and have about a billion boxes to unpack or I'd go crazy. What's your name?

DENNIS Dennis Thompson, age 21, six foot, one sixty. Brown hair, blue eyes.

LISA That's sounds like a police description.

DENNIS On the other side of the law more likely. It's an expository act.

LISA *(Nodding.)* So do you live here alone?

DENNIS Just me and my imaginary friends.

LISA Do you talk to them much?

DENNIS No, they mostly ignore me and go about their lives. I didn't say they were good imaginary friends.

LISA I see. This is my first time moving out by myself. That's kind of strange, I know, moving out for the first time at twenty-four. I lived with a roommate through college and after I graduated I lived with my boyfriend for a while. I always wondered what it would be like, you know?

DENNIS The wonder should wear off in about six or seven years.

LISA How long have you lived here?

DENNIS Two years.

LISA *(Looking behind Dennis.)* Wow, a lot of books. You go to UWM?

DENNIS Nope. No college, just barely high school.

LISA Oh. I went to Parkside got a degree in business.

DENNIS I'm sorry.

LISA *(Nodding.)* Me, too. It seems like everyone else got one, too. Well, I have to be going. The phone company representative should be coming at about ten o'clock.

DENNIS Hope you don't have any plans for the afternoon.

LISA *(Smiling.)* No, just unpacking. And, since I have a lot of it, I'd best get back to it. See you later.

DENNIS See you.

    EXIT LISA.

DENNIS *(Addressing stage right.)* Pretty good. You managed to have her slip in that she was alone and that she and her boyfriend have just broken up. She is free and available this afternoon. And I am supposed to jump at this. Maybe I could have asked to help her unpack and then go out for a bite to eat. She was rather nice, and I'll bet we could have hit it off. I know the old adage "Never look a gift horse in the mouth," but given where the saying comes from, it should probably be "always look the gift horse in the mouth" or something along those lines. Not that Lisa is a horse. Quite far from it. But I am looking at the gift in the mouth and saying, no, you slime, you probably would have me give her the waddles and run away for your sadistic kicks or have her break my heart or something. In any case, it would be you directing me again, and I'm on strike for that very reason. *(Sits back down.)* How long have I been sitting here? I think I just sat down, but how can I be sure? My memory is strange. It's not a continuous series of days, but just highlights. Did you forget to put in everything else? I know I was in Mrs. Walters's second grade class, but I can't remember where I sat. No, wait. I sat next to a kid named Tyrone, in the fourth row and by the coat closet. Bad example. I think I remember waking up this morning and having a cold Pop-Tart for breakfast. *(Gets up and looks in trash can.)* The foil is there, but....There's no way to be sure. Anything I remember could just be thrown in by you right then with the appropriate supporting details. *(Sits again and thinks until there is a knock on the door.)* If that's Lisa again, I'm going to scream. *(Three knocks.)* Time to go. *(Three more knocks.)* Time to go. *(Four knocks.)* Come in!

    ENTER CHRIS.

DENNIS   *(Screams, then addresses audience.)* If you thought you could stop me from screaming just because you put Chris on the other side of the door, you're wrong.

CHRIS   *(Screams too.)* And I'm glad to see you, too. What's up, Dennis?

DENNIS   Not much.

CHRIS   Hey—you've been thinking again. I see it in your face. You better cut that out. You know that thinking kills good brain cells.

DENNIS   You're so frivolous and superficial.

CHRIS   And supercilious and artificial, but that's why you like me. And you're jealous because I can have a good time without wrecking it by picking it apart.

DENNIS   You wouldn't know how to pick anything apart.

CHRIS   And it keeps me happy. Come on, I'm heading down to the beach. You want to come and catch some rays? Maybe scope the bees before you head into the office?

DENNIS   Not today, thanks.

CHRIS   So what have you been thinking about now that's got you all peeved?

DENNIS   You want to see something?

CHRIS   What?

DENNIS   *(Takes a quarter from his pocket and flips.)* What did it come up?

CHRIS   Tails.

DENNIS   I thought so. *(Takes another coin and flips it.)* And this one?

CHRIS   Tails.

DENNIS   *(Takes another coin and flips it.)* Tails again. And again. And again ad infinitum.

CHRIS   Nope, that one was heads.

DENNIS   What? *(Examines coin.)* How did that happen?

CHRIS   What were you going to show me?

DENNIS   How easily amused you were. Watching me flip coins like that. What did you expect to see? Some secret of the universe?

CHRIS   Oh, I see, one of those moods. Okay. Like I said, I'm going to the lakefront. If you want to come, I'll be in our usual spot. See you later.

    EXIT CHRIS.

DENNIS   *(Addressing audience.)* He sounded awfully sure, didn't he? Maybe going to the beach today is a turning point in the action, eh? Too bad I won't be there to support the plot. Just what you'd like— for me to go and romp on Bradford Beach among the girls in bikinis so that I would forget my resolution. A little frisbee, a little volleyball, and I would be blithely back in line on your page. I think not. *(Thinks.)* All I want is control of my own plot. Freedom, I guess you'd call it. I want to be able to run and jump and frolic without it being a side effect of the clack of a typewriter. I don't want to be chained to your stupid literary pretensions. I wouldn't mind even if it were a good action story, with me rescuing ladies from dragons or gangsters, but it had to be one of these droll modernist things where nothing happens, where the entire point is bemoaning how futile life is and how unbelievably dull and lonely it is to be a modern person. I'd like a nice bit of flow, thank you, a building to a climax or series of climaxes in which the entire purpose is made clear. I want a point, damn it. *(Goes to window.)* Sure is a nice day for the beach, though. *(Opens window.)* A nice southerly breeze. I could just leap out of the window and end your book right now. Kill the series character. Kill your chance at selling action figures. Even then I wouldn't be free. I'd be trapped somewhere in the after-life. If there is such of thing, and, of course, if they let fictional characters into it. Besides, your book might turn out to be just a short story tragedy piece. Wouldn't be a very good piece, especially since that sort of thing happens in the world very day. Even with a bit of irony thrown in—the Publisher's Clearinghouse van showing up with cameras and a ten million dollar check for me just in time to catch me trying to cannonball the pavement. It'd make one of those reality shows, but not the commercials. Now for a little reality check, I'm only on the second floor, so I'd probably only end up looking stupid and breaking a leg. Never mind. *(Closes window and begins to pace, but stops before the bookcase.)*

Oh, Ayn, what would you have me do? Go to work and do something manual. No thanks. How about you, Larry? It wouldn't really matter what I did. You'd just take a big rock and ram it into the planet and start a major upheaval. Or you, Phil? It wouldn't matter. Everyone would be against me and reality itself would be a fabrication, and that's hard to stomach. Oh, Fyodor, what would you have me do? Pace about in a little cell and go slowly insane. *(Looks about and addresses audience.)* Well, you're not even that good. What's your racket, bub? *(Waits in silence for a few moments.)* What, no word from you? No thundering voice from heaven that tells me to get on the stick and get on with the action? *(Phone rings.)* A-ha! A thundering voice from heaven via AT&T. *(Phone rings again. Dennis answers.)* Yeah, boss? Who are you? What is the meaning of this call? No, no, what do you really want? Are you the guy writing this or not? Hello? *(Hangs up—Dennis addresses stage right.)* You wanted to sell me storm windows? You know I don't live in my own home, you moron! *(Pauses.)* What if you don't exist, then? What if I am standing here ranting to myself? *(Looks about.)* Well, even if I am, at least there's no one to hear me. I'd hate to think how silly I'd look wandering around my apartment talking foolish. *(Clunking from stage left. Dennis thinks.)* I wonder if he's given up on me. I don't feel him pulling any strings. Maybe it worked—maybe he gave me the equivalent of my fictional character walking papers. I didn't here or feel any twang of him letting go, but I don't suppose that I would. *(Paces.)* Come to think of it, I have been doing pretty much anything I wanted to after I said I was going on strike. *(Raises arm.)* I wanted to do that, and I don't think it would serve any purpose in the plot of a novel for me to do that. *(Raises other arm and flaps them.)* Well, I'm not flying, so I guess the laws of reality apply. *(Dances a rather uncoordinated jig.)* Full motor control, well, as well as can be expected. We'll have to try some major plot revisions. First thing will be to learn to dance. *(Knock on the door.)* Who is it?

LISA   *(From without.)* Your new neighbor.

DENNIS   *(Aside.)* Now for some major plot revisions. *(Opens door.)*

    ENTER LISA.

LISA   Can you believe it? The phone man, the cable man, and the Sears people all came at the same time.

DENNIS   On the day they said they would?

LISA   No, actually the cable man was supposed to come tomorrow.

DENNIS   No way.

LISA   Way.

DENNIS   What are the odds of that happening? It must be your day. Did you buy a lottery ticket today?

LISA   *(Nodding.)* No, but I probably should. Anyway, I've come to ask a favor. With the cable guy trying to sell me pay channels and the phone man asking me where I wanted the second jack, I managed to have the Sears guys put the refrigerator in the wrong place. They put it where the dishwasher is supposed to go, so I was wondering if you could help me scoot it over about three feet.

DENNIS   Well, my afternoon happens to be free.

LISA   It shouldn't take that long.

DENNIS   Oh, I know, but I hoped that maybe afterwards you would reward me by accompanying me to lunch. I know this charming little sidewalk cafe where we can grab a bite and then while away the afternoon drinking sodas and watching the people go by.

LISA   A sidewalk cafe?

DENNIS   Okay, it's really a fast-food joint with plastic tables outside. Or we could go down to the lakefront. I know this really nice spot down on the beach, with a commanding view of Lake Michigan and the snack bar. What do you say?

LISA   Is the sidewalk cafe a McDonald's?

DENNIS   Indeed, McDonald's it tis, me bonnie lass. Let us move your refrigerator. *(Aside.)* Rescuing maidens from misplaced refrigerators is a start, and a lot safer.

LISA   I didn't mean to interrupt a phone call.

DENNIS   What do you mean?

LISA   I heard you talking. Were you on the phone?

DENNIS   Er, no, I was just reciting a dramatic soliloquy from a play.

LISA   What play?

DENNIS   Oh, a little thing. You've probably never heard of it.

EXEUNT.

The End

About the Author

Brian J. Noggle graduated from Marquette University with a degree in Writing Intensive English and hoped to make his fortune as a writer. Fortunately, he was able to find a real job when he discovered his writing paychecks were meager and infrequent. He has worked in the Information Technology industry for over a decade but has continued to write for magazines occasionally. He lives near Springfield, Missouri, with his wife, children, and cats as well as the coyotes, turkeys, raccoons, skunks, skinks, rat snakes, armadillos, and other wee beasties that have so far agreed not to eat him.

www.ingramcontent.com/pod-product-compliance
Lightning Source LLC
Chambersburg PA
CBHW021218020426
42331CB00003B/355